11/19 1

A Lawyer's Guide to the
ALEXANDER TECHNIQUE

A Lawyer's Guide to the
ALEXANDER TECHNIQUE

*Using Your Mind-Body Connection
to Handle Stress, Alleviate Pain and
Improve Performance*

Karen G. Krueger

Printed in the United States of America.

19 18 17 16 15 5 4 3 2 1

Library of Congress Cataloging-in-Publication Data

Krueger, Karen G., author.
  A lawyer's guide to the Alexander technique : using your mind-body connection to handle stress, alleviate pain, and improve performance / Karen G. Krueger.
      pages cm
  Includes bibliographical references and index.
  ISBN 978-1-62722-593-9 (alk. paper)
  1. Lawyers—Life skills guides. 2. Lawyers—United States. 3. Alexander technique. 4. Exercise therapy—United States. 5. Posture. 6. Mind and body—United States. I. Title.
  KF297.K78 2015
  340.023'73—dc23
                                                                    2015034395
Discounts are available for books ordered in bulk. Special consideration is given to state bars, CLE programs, and other bar-related organizations. Inquire at Book Publishing, ABA Publishing, American Bar Association, 321 N. Clark Street, Chicago, Illinois 60654-7598.

www.ShopABA.org

Contents

List of Photos

Acknowledgments

I would like to thank my editor, Jonathan Malysiak, for suggesting that I write this book and supporting me throughout the process; Peter Wald, for taking the wonderful photographs; Anastasia Pridlides, for her help with the diagram on page 47; and Joseph P. McDonnell and Helen Farmer, for so ably and beautifully posing as lawyers (which they certainly are not!).

For their support, encouragement, and contributions to my learning, I would also like to thank the faculty and my fellow members of the Board of Directors of the American Center for the Alexander Technique; all my past and present teachers, including my mentor and current teacher, Judy Stern; my exchange partners Dan Cayer, Michael Hanko, and Anastasia Pridlides; and all my present and former students, lawyers and nonlawyers alike. This book is filled with discoveries we have made together.

Introduction

This book came about through an interview I did with Spencer Mazyck for "Stealth Lawyer," a Bloomberg Law series about lawyers who are no longer practicing law. In my case, Spencer wanted to know why I quit "Big Law" and got involved with something mysterious called the Alexander Technique—and also, as it turned out, he wanted to know what this Alexander Technique was all about. The interview prompted Jonathan Malysiak of ABA Publishing to contact me to see if I would be interested in writing this book.

My first reaction was to think to myself, "The world doesn't need another book about the Alexander Technique." Many good books about the technique already exist. In any case, I believe that books are a feeble substitute for in-person, hands-on work with a trained teacher of the Alexander Technique. Books are a useful adjunct to such work, but I wondered if I really had anything new and different to say.

But on further reflection, I decided that it would be worthwhile to write a book aimed at lawyers and others who work in similar high-skill, high-stress occupations. The Alexander Technique is best known in this country among performing artists, who are often exposed to it during their training. (It is a required part of the curriculum at such institutions as The Julliard School and the Yale School of Drama.) But I rarely encounter someone from the worlds of law, finance, and business who has heard of the Alexander Technique—and when I do, it usually turns out that he or she has a connection to the performing arts, such as a relative who is an actor, a dancer, or a musician.

I have long believed that the Alexander Technique would be of enormous benefit to lawyers, bankers, and business people if only they knew about it. My background—my twenty-five-year career as a lawyer—gives me some credibility with this potential audience. And I am able to speak and write about the technique in ways that make sense to people with similar educational and professional backgrounds to my own. The response to my interview demonstrated that.

Most lawyers think and speak of the mind and the body as two separate aspects of themselves. We tend to erect a wall between mind and body, and most lawyers spend most of their time living on the mental side. The Alexander Technique knocks down that wall. In fact, it asserts that the wall is a fiction—a dangerous fiction that is a major contributor to back pain, neck pain, repetitive strain injuries, headaches, anxiety, insomnia, and many other problems that the Alexander Technique addresses.

The Alexander Technique teaches how the mind—our conscious thinking process—can be used to bring about beneficial changes in how we function physically, mentally, and emotionally. Because thinking is the primary tool of the technique, it is an ideal method for lawyers and other highly educated people to handle stress, alleviate pain, and improve performance. It is, moreover, very practical. It does not require that you believe in any particular philosophy or any elusive concept like chakras or energy (though it does not require that you abandon any such belief, either). Rather, it emphasizes practical experience and experimentation as a way to bring about beneficial changes in yourself.

Sometimes the technique can seem mysterious, both in the way people talk about it and in the way it feels in the moment. I enjoy the mysterious feelings, but I tend to get impatient with the mysterious talking. I like things to make sense, and I like to explain the technique to others in ways that make sense to them. This book contains my current best efforts at clearly explaining what I know about the Alexander Technique.

The substance of what I have to say comes largely from those who have taught me, including my first Alexander Technique teacher, Jessica Wolf, and my current teacher, Judy Stern; the faculty at the American Center for the Alexander Technique, where I trained and received my teacher certification; the colleagues with whom I exchange ideas and hands-on practice; and my students, from whom I learn every time we meet. All of these rich sources have informed my understanding and my teaching.

What follows is my personal perspective on the Alexander Technique: its origins, the basic concepts and skills that it teaches, how it enabled me to overcome chronic pain and feel better than I had dreamed possible, and what it can do for anyone who is inquisitive and persistent enough to spend some time working with a teacher. I hope it will inspire my readers to seek out a personal experience of the Alexander Technique.

CHAPTER 1

This Is about How You Handle Yourself in Life

Enthusiasts for the Alexander Technique report an astonishingly varied and comprehensive collection of physical, mental, emotional, and spiritual problems it has solved and benefits it has provided. For me, though, it started with one simple conundrum: how to stop tensing my neck and shoulders every time the phone in my office rang.

My desire to stop engaging in this common habit had a very practical source. I was suffering from chronic neck pain and headaches, which were interfering with my work as a partner at a major New York law firm. I had never had a particularly keen kinesthetic sense. I had never been athletic, and for much of my adult life, I focused on academic and professional achievement, paying attention to my body only when it demanded food or sleep. Eventually, however, pain forced me to notice things that I had previously ignored. I became aware of my habit of creating tension in my neck and shoulders in response to every ringing telephone and urgent e-mail. Once I noticed this, it was obvious that this habit was contributing to—and maybe even causing—my pain.

Initially, this insight proved less useful than you might think. Although I knew what not to do, I was unable to stop. When I reached the point where I was frequently prevented by pain from doing my work, I took a disability leave, removing myself from the environment in which my habits of tension were so strongly triggered and devoting myself to trying to get better.

I had already consulted many doctors and tried many medications, none of which worked and most of which actually made my condition worse. During my leave, I turned to various other approaches, including physical therapy, swimming, walking, yoga, massage, and meditation. These methods provided some temporary relief, but the pain always returned. It seemed to me that I could not possibly return to any kind of productive work, when I was frequently in pain despite spending almost all of my waking hours taking care of myself.

At this stage in my journey, I was unaware that over a century before, a Tasmanian-born actor named F. M. Alexander (1869–1955) had faced a similar conundrum and had developed a technique to solve it. His problem was not chronic pain, but chronic vocal fatigue—a serious problem for a young man who had already had some success as a reciter of Shakespearean monologues. The story of how he went about analyzing his problem and solving it has been told and retold in many books about the Alexander Technique. His own account, written many years later and published as the first chapter of his book *The Use of the Self*, is the most interesting, not so much as a literal story of what happened, but as his distillation of his discoveries as he came to understand them through years of work on his own and teaching others.

Alexander describes two related problems that emerged as his acting career began to flourish. First, during performances, his voice would become hoarse, and sometimes it failed altogether. Second, friends told him that the quality of his performances was marred by his habit of audibly gasping as though he were sucking in air. He consulted doctors and voice trainers. In addition to undergoing unspecified medical treatments, he was counselled to rest his voice by not speaking and to have surgery to shorten his uvula. He rejected the latter advice, but followed the first, with only limited success. Like my pain, Alexander's hoarseness went away for a time, but returned when he resumed his professional activities.

As Alexander tells the story, the turning point came when, on the advice of his doctor, he accepted an important engagement and, for the two weeks leading up to the performance, faithfully followed the doctor's treatment plan. His voice was strong at the start of the performance, but halfway through the performance, it had begun to be hoarse, and by the end he could hardly speak.

When he talked the matter over with his doctor afterward, he suggested that he must be doing something to himself during his performances that strained his voice. The doctor agreed that this seemed likely, but neither of them had any idea what he might be doing. So Alexander embarked on an odyssey of self-examination and experimentation, in which he discovered the habits that were damaging his voice and developed a technique to change those habits. He then began to teach others the same system, discovering wide-ranging benefits for health and performance. He moved to London and spent time in the United States before and during World War II. On both continents, he and his work became very well known and popular, with various famous adherents like George

Bernard Shaw, Aldous Huxley, and John Dewey. He also trained others to teach his work, and those first-generation teachers continued training others in the United Kingdom, the United States, and elsewhere.

To discover what he was doing to himself to cause his vocal problems, Alexander observed himself in mirrors while reciting and also while speaking normally. He first noticed that when he recited, he did three things that seemed to be problematic: "I tended to pull back the head, depress the larynx and suck in breath through the mouth in such a way as to produce a gasping sound." (*The Use of the Self*, Orion Books Ltd. 2001, p. 26.) Next, he observed that he did subtler versions of the same things when speaking normally. Eventually, he discovered that if he refrained from pulling his head back, the other two habits subsided as well, and his voice became less hoarse. He experimented with various head positions and other postural changes until he settled on an optimum "use of himself" (to use his language).

Alexander concluded, based on these experiments and his lifelong work teaching his technique to others, that the relationship among the head, neck, and back is the primary determiner of overall coordination, for good or for ill. He came to refer to this as the "primary control."

He also made two other discoveries with very practical consequences: first, that merely knowing it would be better not to pull his head back was not sufficient to enable him to refrain from doing so in a real-life situation such as reciting; and second, that he could not rely on what he felt to determine what he was actually doing. Even after he developed a way to practice not pulling his head back while reciting, he often felt that he had succeeded, only to observe in his mirrors that he had failed. With persistence and patience, he honed his technique and tested it on himself, until he was able to use it to change his own harmful habits and then to teach others to do the same.

I have personally experienced the reality of Alexander's discoveries. I had a habit of contracting the muscles of my neck, shoulders, and back in response to various stimuli: ringing telephones, but also working at my computer, negotiating, reading, exercising, and talking. In fact, I tensed up to do just about anything, though at first I only noticed when tension became pain. In Alexander's terms, I was misusing my "primary control." My ability to perceive this habit in action was quite limited, but when I tensed my neck at the sound of the phone, the immediate increase in pain made the connection obvious to me before I ever heard of Alexander and his technique.

I shared this observation with the various experts whose help I sought. My doctor prescribed muscle relaxants and physical therapy. My physical therapists and my yoga instructor suggested changes in my posture and body alignment in specific exercises and poses. The exercise and attention to my body, under their guidance, did provide some pain relief. According to my physical therapists, stretching and strengthening my muscles would also correct my bad habits. But each time I went back to normal, stressful activities, the pain would return, and I would realize, too late, that the tension in my neck, shoulders, and back had reappeared.

It was at this point that I first learned about the Alexander Technique from a friend who had had lessons many years earlier. Hearing that I was struggling with pain centered in my neck muscles and the base of my skull, she told me that "the Alexander Technique has a lot to do with that part of the body" and suggested I read a book called *Body Learning: An Introduction to the Alexander Technique*, by Michael J. Gelb. I had read only a few pages before I decided that I had to try this technique, which purported to teach how to change harmful habits of posture and movement. I found a teacher and began weekly lessons.

Thus began a process of gradual improvement. At first, I was in pain much of the time; I now believe that I had a repetitive strain injury in my neck that needed to heal. As a consequence, much of my body was braced, and my already dull kinesthetic sense was further dampened, so that I felt mainly pain or the absence of pain. I had to slowly let go of the protective mechanisms I had built to deal with the pain and reawaken my ability to sense what was happening in my body and where it was in space, so that I could relearn how to sit, stand, move, and deal with everyday activities. As my posture and movement improved, my pain lessened and the episodes became less frequent. After 4 months, I returned to work part-time and continued my weekly lessons with my Alexander Technique teacher.

Along the way, I learned many things that astonished me. For example, I discovered that learning to avoid creating unnecessary tension in my neck and shoulders made me a more effective negotiator. It also improved my balance on cross-country skis and ice skates. The link between these seemingly unconnected skills was what Alexander called the "primary control."

Many of us live too much of our lives in a state of startled reactivity, which adversely affects our physical, mental, and emotional functioning. This diminished functioning takes many forms, such as physical pain, anxiety, stomach upset, and insomnia. These dysfunctions add to the stress and distress of life, further reinforcing the patterns of reaction.

To give a simple example, suppose I am representing a company seeking to acquire another company. The lawyer representing the target company has a way of getting under my skin every time we speak; even simple matters turn into protracted arguments. I'm about to call this lawyer on the phone, and I'm feeling anxious about how the conversation will go. I'm anticipating the angry, frustrated feelings that I will have as I try to break through his unreasonable positioning. As I think ahead to this unpleasant phone call, I start to tense my neck and shoulders and to hold my breath. When I don't breathe freely, I get less oxygen than I need. This lack of oxygen does not feel good, and I interpret the feeling as anxiety, making myself feel even worse. My neck and shoulders tighten further as I steep in my own anxiety.

Alexander developed a way to stop this vicious circle by interrupting its physical manifestations, using conscious awareness and thought. In the scenario sketched above, having learned in my Alexander Technique lessons to notice the physical reactions associated with my thoughts and emotions, I first pause in the process of getting ready for my phone call and consider how my mental and emotional state is affecting my body. Perceiving that I am holding my breath, I let it out and allow a new breath to come in. I also realize that excess tension has built up in my neck and shoulders, and I think about releasing it. Because I have practiced this process many times with the help of my teacher, it has a noticeable effect: my breathing resumes and my neck and shoulders become less tense. These changes lessen my perception of anxiety, enabling me to release more tension and continue to breathe more freely. I can now pick up the phone and call my adversary in a frame of mind and body that is more conducive to keeping my cool when he provokes me in his accustomed manner. I can even renew my thinking to continue breathing and releasing tension in my neck and shoulders during the phone call.

This process may sound mysterious, but it is actually quite straightforward. I believe that anyone who is willing and able to practice can learn it, with the right instruction. Certainly anyone with the intelligence, drive, and persistence that it takes to be a successful lawyer can learn the Alexander Technique.

Only a few weeks before I wrote these words, a lawyer student of mine reported using the technique to calm his reactions to a task at work that was giving him difficulties, and finding that suddenly it became much easier to accomplish what he needed to do. This student had initially come for lessons to deal with a specific physical pain, but like me and many others, has found that the Alexander Technique has the potential to improve performance and functioning in many different ways.

Another student of mine once exclaimed at the end of a particularly productive lesson, "This is about how you handle yourself in life!" In that moment, she had had an insight into the broad implications of Alexander's discoveries. But for most people—including me, initially—the motivation to learn more about the Alexander Technique is both more mundane and more urgent: a need to be healthier, more efficient, and more effective in the activities of daily life.

Consider whether, in the course of your workday, you do any of the following:

- Slouch and crane your neck forward at your desk
- Pull your shoulders up toward your ears
- Pound on your computer keyboard using the full force of your arms
- Pull your sternum up and push your shoulders back to try to sit up straight
- Manipulate the pitch and volume of your voice to sound more authoritative
- Push your head up and down for emphasis as you speak
- Sit on your tailbone
- Strain your eyes, neck, and shoulders to see your computer screen
- Hold your phone between your ear and your shoulder
- Crouch over your smartphone and tighten your arms while typing with your thumbs

Now consider whether you experience any of the following:

- Neck pain
- Headaches
- Lower back pain
- Carpal tunnel syndrome
- Eyestrain
- Hoarseness and vocal fatigue
- Breathing difficulties
- General fatigue
- Anxiety
- Insomnia

Is there a connection between the habits in the first list and the problems in the second? Could changing the habits ameliorate the problems? And how would you go about changing the habits? The Alexander Technique provides a way to find out.

CHAPTER 2

"You Debunk Everything!"

Some time ago, a young legal recruiter came to me for her first experience of the Alexander Technique. She was a former dancer, with the posture to show for it: she had the classic ballet dancer's stance, with sternum raised, shoulders held back, and head held high. She was first astonished, and then delighted, when I helped her find an easier way to stand upright. It was clearly a great relief to her to discover that good posture could feel so good. Toward the end of the lesson, she turned to me and exclaimed, "You debunk everything!"

Learning the Alexander Technique does require considering the possibility that many common beliefs may not be correct. Here are a number of examples that we will explore:

- Your belief about what your body is doing and where it is in space may not be accurate.
- What you think is "good posture" can be as bad for you as "bad posture."
- "Keeping your eyes on the prize" can be counterproductive; focusing too hard on your goal may actually interfere with attaining it.
- The Cartesian view that mind and body are separate is incorrect: thoughts exist in the body and thinking can change your physical state.
- Reacting quickly to all demands for action (including demands you make on yourself) can be harmful.
- You can't "project" your voice.
- You shouldn't "take a deep breath."
- Doing nothing is not a waste of time.

In my teaching practice, I get to know my students in a very specific but profound way. They generally come seeking a means to feel better and healthier or to change a habit that they don't like. In the process of seeking change, we discover their fundamental beliefs about how the body and mind work, what improved functioning actually entails, and how to achieve it. Often, we discover that my point of view about these questions differs from theirs.

Some of these differences are simply a matter of information. Most people don't know much about anatomy, either in general or in relation to their own bodies, and much of what they think they know is wrong. I teach them where to find the top of their spines, their hip joints, their wrists and ankles, and so forth, not just in a picture or model skeleton, but in themselves. I teach them about the movements of bone, muscle, and other tissues throughout the torso that occur with each breath. I show them how simple actions, such as rising from a chair, can be done more easily and efficiently with some simple changes in mechanics.

Information alone, however, does not necessarily result in change. I once helped to introduce a large group of advanced physical therapy students to the Alexander Technique. They all knew much more about anatomy than I do. Unlike most people, they were already quite familiar with the location of the atlanto-occipital (AO) joint. (You can see a diagram showing the AO joint on page 47.) In fact, they had been taught to teach patients to do what they called the "AO nod," that is, the subtle movement of the head on the AO joint that is like nodding "yes." (Alexander Technique teachers also work on this movement with their students.) However, when I went around the room putting my hands on the heads of these highly trained students and worked with them on nodding in this way, not one of them was actually able to move the head freely on the AO joint; their necks were all far too tense to allow for the freedom Alexander Technique teachers seek to elicit.

It is important for most people to understand some basic facts about their anatomy, such as where the major joints are, in order to make more efficient use of themselves. But my students and I also discover and examine their beliefs about other physical "facts" about posture, movement, breathing, and voice—which are often of dubious accuracy and utility.

I often find myself needing to clarify for my students what we are aiming for, exactly, in our lessons. This goes beyond posture and mechanics. Many people, especially many successful lawyers and other professionals, live in a state of almost constant muscle tension. Learning to move out of this state in Alexander Technique lessons is a huge relief. At any given time, I seem to have at least a few students whose main reason for taking time and spending money to have lessons with me is the "table work" that we do, during which the student lies on my table: it seems to be the only regular opportunity some people give themselves to relax and let go of having to be busy all the time.

This can give rise to the idea that the Alexander Technique is about relaxation, which is only partly right. Muscles that are overworking do need to do less. However, usually when some part of the body is overworking, another part is underworking. Thus, the rebalancing that happens in Alexander Technique lessons may involve inducing some muscles to have increased tone while others have decreased tone.

Many people say they feel more relaxed than usual during and after their Alexander Technique lessons. When I ask them what specific feelings they are noticing, they may report feeling lighter, more energetic, or less tense. They associate this pleasant experience with situations that are relaxing—with a good long vacation, for example. Thus, they interpret the sensations they are feeling in their bodies as indicating that they are relaxed. There's nothing wrong with this label, unless it brings other mental baggage with it. If you think that the Alexander Technique requires that you relax, and you also think that you can't be relaxed and work hard at the same time, or that you can only relax when you lie down and close your eyes, you will have trouble using Alexander Technique skills at the office. So I tend not to speak about relaxation to my students, but rather about releasing unnecessary tension and muscle work. Telling someone to relax is generally counterproductive anyway. Or, as I often tell my students, "trying to relax" is an oxymoron. You can't relax by trying hard.

You also can't recreate a feeling by "memorizing" it or trying to feel your way back to it. Once I tried to explain this to a friend, and she came up with this analogy: if you are feeling sad or stressed, and think back to being really happy when you were on vacation, the memory might make you might feel briefly better, but if you want to really re-experience that feeling, you must re-create the conditions that gave rise to it. When I help a student to use the Alexander Technique skills that we are practicing together to create a feeling of ease in movement with less neck tension, that feeling is usually clear and memorable, and my student will recognize it next time it arises. When the student closes her eyes and says "I want to try to remember how this feels and hold onto it," she is not really at risk of forgetting what it feels like. Rather, she means something like "I want to hold this position and remember it so I can get this great feeling back on my own." But the position didn't create the feeling, and "holding onto" a position or a feeling results in stiffening and tension. You'll never feel exactly the same thing twice. If you want to keep revisiting that place of ease and enjoyment in movement, you can—by going through the process again.

This emphasis on process is at the heart of the matter. When we speak of "learning" in this context, we are talking about learning a skill, not learning information. When I first took Alexander lessons, I noticed that my teacher repeated the same information, the same phrases, over and over. I wondered if she thought I was stupid. I didn't have to be told twice to think of allowing my neck to be free or to bend my hips, knees, and ankles to sit down.

Later, I discovered that I did have to be told twice—or rather, hundreds of times. The words she was using were not merely concepts and information for me to learn intellectually. Rather, they were thoughts to live by, to live with in my body. Every once in a while, the embodied experience I had under her hands matched with the words in a new way, and suddenly I had a whole new understanding of something I had heard many times before.

Learning the Alexander Technique is the opposite of an all-or-nothing proposition. You will not always do everything "right" from an Alexander Technique perspective—nor is it necessary. You don't have to quit your "bad" postural habits cold turkey. In fact, the whole "right–wrong" paradigm is useless in this endeavor. I'm more interested in helping my students discover how they do things and try out new ways to see if they prefer them. It's more productive than looking for mistakes, and it's more enjoyable.

It can take a while before I can persuade a new student to take this attitude of discovery and nonjudgment. After all, they usually come to me to solve a problem, and they want to be told what to do and when they go wrong. They are mostly people who have been extremely successful at school and careers, and they want to do well at this, too. It's part of who they are.

I'm not saying that my students shouldn't have goals, or that they shouldn't seek my guidance in how to attain them. But the vocabulary of "right–wrong," "good–bad," and "should–shouldn't" that frames so much of our lives has a strong tendency to evoke the very reactions that we are seeking to interrupt and change. Many of us experience being scolded, yelled at, and told what to do by authority figures from a young age. Those of us who were good students and well-behaved children (and I am one of them) learned how to avoid these experiences and gain praise and rewards by being extremely responsive, always ready and eager to please. Those behaviors and attitudes continue to serve us in adulthood, especially in highly demanding careers such as practicing law. And those behaviors and attitudes often come with a built-in, automatic muscle set: tense neck and shoulders, tight back muscles, and all the other attributes of the startle pattern that we will examine in the next chapter.

Envision a school-aged child being reprimanded by a teacher for not completing his homework: if the child cares at all about doing well at school, or about having the teacher's approval, he will freeze, tense up, and cringe. As adults, we freeze, tense up, and cringe in response to the admonitions in our own heads: "I should finish writing this brief before I leave the office." "Work through your fatigue, because this has to get done before morning." "I promised this to the client by the end of the week, and I can't fail to deliver." "My feelings of worry and anxiety demonstrate that I am being appropriately thorough in my research." "If I don't look intense enough, my colleagues will think I am not taking this project seriously." "I can't afford to make a single mistake."

These attitudes represent the drive and perfectionism that motivate many lawyers. However, the Alexander Technique does not require perfection. Indeed it requires a willingness to make mistakes, to be uncertain, and to be experimental, as part of the process of learning. Anyone who has learned to play a sport or a musical instrument knows that repetitive practice is necessary to gain skill and mastery, and practice entails making mistakes as well as getting it right. Learning the Alexander Technique is like that.

Another comparable experience is learning a foreign language. There is grammar to assimilate and vocabulary to learn. But to actually speak, read, and comprehend the language, you have to practice. At first, you practice simple, repetitive exercises that seem stilted, as your mind, ear, and tongue become accustomed to the new sounds and meanings. This phase is like going to Alexander Technique lessons and sitting down and standing up again, over and over. Later, you are able to improvise in your new language: you begin to understand actual people saying spontaneous things, and you can express your own thoughts in the moment. As an Alexander student, you begin to be able to apply the skills you are learning to real-life situations as they arise. Finally, if you persist, you become comfortable functioning in your new language, and may even think and dream in it occasionally. As an Alexander student, you eventually find that your new way of being has become habitual, displacing the old, damaging habits that you wished to discard. What previously you could do only with full attention, when there were no outside pressures, has now become a part of you.

CHAPTER 3

The Force of Habit

As I said earlier, many lawyers exist in a state of almost constant muscle tension and react to the demands of others and of the voices in their heads by freezing, tensing up, and cringing. All of us have a tendency to respond to any strong stimulus by tightening all of our muscles in a way that pulls our heads down onto our spines and our limbs into our torsos. In most cases, however, it would be better to do the opposite: to sit, stand, move, and speak with a lengthening spine and a general expansion of the whole body.

To understand what I mean, consider the photographs on the following pages. The man who is slouching forward has had to overly contract the muscles in the back of his neck in order to hold his head up enough to see his computer screen. As a result, the weight of his head is pressing down on his spine, and the weight of his upper torso is compressing him downward. This posture puts strain on the muscles of the neck and back and restricts breathing. In the second photo, he sits upright with the weight of his head balanced on the top of his spine, allowing all the muscles of his torso to work as they should to keep him upright.

The woman who is slumping backward may appear relaxed, but she too must tense her neck muscles and push her head forward in order to see her computer. In addition, the weight of her head and upper torso presses on her lower back and tailbone. Again, when she sits upright, the weight of her head is easily supported by her torso on a lengthening spine.

In the photo on page 18, we see illustrated a very common way people interact with their electronic devices: head pushed forward and arms contracted into the body. She holds a great deal of tension in her shoulders and neck, both to support the off-balance weight of her head and because her arms and hands are excessively tight.

Slouching forward

Sitting upright

Slumping backward

Sitting upright

Clutching the smartphone

All of these ways of "misusing" ourselves (to use Alexander's jargon) have in common that the head is out of balance and the neck muscles are overly tight. The head is heavy, and it's important for survival that it not hit the ground. When the postural reflexes are working properly, the head balances relatively easily on the top of the spine. However, when things are out of balance, your muscles work harder to keep you from falling. And generally this happens without your having to think about it.

For example, imagine you are walking at a brisk pace down a city sidewalk. As your right foot hits the ground and your left foot begins to swing forward, you catch your left toe on a slightly raised piece of cement. Your forward momentum is checked, but your head is already slightly ahead of your center of balance. If your stride had not been interrupted, your left foot would have come forward to take the weight of your head and propel it on. Instead, your head is now off-balance with nothing to keep it from falling forward. If you are lucky, though, before you even realize precisely what is happening, your neck and back muscles will contract, pulling your head back and allowing you to recover your footing without falling.

The Startle Reflex

One name for this automatic reaction is the startle reflex. It is familiar to all of us. Just recall what happens when you are surprised by a sudden loud noise: your neck tightens, your shoulders pull up, your arms and legs contract into your body. This has its uses. As noted above, it can help you avoid falling when you are suddenly taken off-balance. It is also a typical response to sudden danger.

Once when I was hiking in California, I suddenly found myself frozen in a classic startle pose. It was a few seconds before I realized that there was a rattlesnake curled up three feet ahead of me on the path. Had I continued to walk, rather than freezing even before I became consciously aware of the snake, I might well have stepped on it. I remained rooted to the ground while I considered what to do. Eventually, the snake slithered away, and I continued my hike, though it was a good hour before I calmed down and undid the chain reaction of muscle tension and adrenaline that this automatic reflex unleashed.

It was a good thing that I had that reflex in reaction to the very real danger of the snake in my path. It is less useful to have the same reaction to a ringing phone or an angry client. It is downright unhealthy to become so habituated to your reactions to stress that you never really entirely let go of the muscle tension that it brings about. I lived for years with excess muscle tension and the related poor posture, and only began to be aware of it when it caused me pain.

The startle reflex

Alexander's vocal problems were caused by his version of the same pattern. In response to the stimulus—we might call it the stress—of performing, he tightened the muscles of his neck in such a way as to pull his head down onto his spine, thus putting pressure on his vocal mechanism and making it harder to breathe naturally. This habit caused both the vocal strain that troubled him and the gasping for air that detracted from the quality of his performances.

Unlearning Habits: The Alexander Technique Skills

In the first chapter, I described the difficulty that Alexander and I both confronted after realizing that our problems were caused by certain bad habits. It comes down to this: when we are used to moving, sitting, and standing in a particular habitual way, it feels strange, even wrong, to move, sit, and stand differently. We may be able to change when our attention is focused on making the change, but as soon as our attention is taken up with something else, habit takes over. It takes time, repetition, and thought to make the new way of doing things habitual enough to sustain in normal activity.

When I begin working with a new student, I give him or her a short document I have written summarizing everything I will teach him or her in a course of lessons (see Appendix 1). How any given person comes to truly understand and embody these skills and concepts is extremely individual. I teach through words, visual aids, mental images, touch, and movement, and gradually my student and I discover how to make the skills and concepts part of the student's daily life. Words alone are rarely sufficient to enable us to put the Alexander Technique into practice, but I have found that lawyers and other people who are highly analytical often appreciate having a conceptual framework for the experiences they have in lessons. I will summarize these concepts here and develop them in more detail in the succeeding chapters.

The skills that the Alexander Technique teaches are called, in our jargon, *awareness*, *inhibition*, and *direction*. *Awareness* is noticing habitual movement patterns and reactions. For example, before I took lessons, I had already become aware that I tightened the muscles of my neck and shoulders when the phone rang. Through my lessons, I began to be able to notice that the same thing happened frequently and in many different activities. Alexander Technique teachers are highly trained observers of this kind of habit, using their eyes, their touch, and even their ears to discover how their students go about everyday activities like sitting, standing, breathing, and talking. They then assist their students to become more aware of their own habits in activity.

The second Alexander Technique skill, *inhibition*, requires some definition. Alexander did not use this term in the psychological sense of unhealthy repression. Rather, he meant inhibition of one's first reaction to a stimulus to act, taking enough time to be able to carry out the action in a nonhabitual way. The stimulus to act may come from outside or inside, but in either case the Alexander Technique asks that we pause briefly before responding. For example, when my cell phone rings, I can pause for a moment before I pick it up to answer. In this pause, I may become aware that my neck and shoulder muscles are already beginning to tense in anticipation of the action of reaching for the phone. This gives me the opportunity to decide to stop doing that and respond in a different way.

Direction, the third skill, is the practice of giving instructions to oneself about how to carry out any action. Alexander came up with a set of instructions, which have been written in various formulations. One version I like to use is to think to myself:

> I allow my neck to be free;
> So that my head can release forward and up (away from the top of my spine);
> So that my whole torso can lengthen and widen;
> So that my knees can release forward and away from my torso;
> So that my heels can release back and down;
> So that my neck can be free. . . . etc.

These words are of limited utility without an actual embodied experience of what they mean. I have found that there are as many ways to express these ideas as there are different individuals.

What Interferes with Change? The Alexander Technique Concepts

There are many reasons that habits are difficult to change. Alexander identified two that he called "debauched kinesthesia" and "end-gaining."

"Debauched kinesthesia" is a term Alexander used for the situation when what a person believes he is doing, based on his feeling sense, is not objectively accurate. (He also used the more prosaic term "unreliable sensory appreciation" for this phenomenon.) It is easy for an Alexander Technique teacher to make a student aware of how his or her feeling sense is inaccurate. Typically, a new student comes with a particular way that he or she usually stands. The following photos show some variations.

The sloucher   "Standing up straight"   Easily upright

Often, the person who stands as in the middle photo is a reformed sloucher. The middle posture is also common with dancers and yoga practitioners, whose training often includes instructions to carry themselves this way. However, both postures are in fact less than ideal.

It is probably more obvious to you why the slouch is a bad idea. The sloucher allows the weight of her head to press down on her spine, compressing her whole torso, including her lungs and other organs. She has locked her right knee and her torso is collapsed and compressed downward, particularly on the right side.

When she "stands up straight," by contrast, she uses a great deal of muscle effort to lift her chest, pull her shoulders back and straighten her neck. Her back is shortened, putting pressure into her lower back, and overworking her shoulder muscles. Many people believe that this is "good posture." In fact, however, this posture distorts the spine as much as its opposite, the slouch. Both of them also interfere with easy head balance and breathing.

The photo on the right shows what emerges when an Alexander Technique teacher introduces a third way: You can see that she is now standing upright with her head balanced at the top of her body. However, almost invariably, when I help a new student go from slouching or "standing up straight" to this way of standing, he or she will not feel straight. Instead, the sloucher will exclaim, "I feel like I'm leaning backwards." And his counterpart, the "good-posture" aficionado, will exclaim, "But you have me slouching!" A glance in the mirror suffices to show them each how wrong they are.

In the next chapter, we'll examine this phenomenon in greater detail, discussing why and how we become unable to determine accurately what we are doing and how the Alexander Technique addresses the problem.

"End-gaining" is Alexander's term for another key concept of his technique. Alexander observed that people often allow their desire to achieve a particular goal to predominate over any consideration of how best to go about working toward it. They think that having conceived a goal, sheer hard work will allow them to achieve it. If they meet with failure, they just work harder, instead of considering the possibility that they need to try a new approach. Alexander discovered this in himself. At first, when he realized that he should stop pulling his head back and down when he spoke or recited, he assumed that that realization would suffice to enable him to "gain" that "end" (to use his terms). However, this proved wrong. In fact, he had to set aside his strong desire to change this habit and work out a process to use to retrain himself. He called this the "means whereby" his goal could be attained.

This concept is at the core of Alexander Technique lessons. Teachers have their students engage in simple activities, like going from sitting to standing and back again, with their attention on not what they are doing, but how they are doing it. We may even use Alexander's terms, asking a student to "stop end-gaining and pay attention to the means-whereby." This is not to say that the Alexander Technique requires giving up having goals. Rather, it asks you to consider the possibility that excessive attention to a goal can actually interfere with working out the best way to attain it.

A Note on Furniture and Ergonomics

Many of my students ask me what kind of desk chair they should use. My standard answer is that the best chair in the world will not ensure that you sit well, but a bad chair can make it impossible. A chair that is too big or too small for you, or that has a very soft seat, a seat that slants backward, arms that make it hard not to raise your shoulders, a lumbar "support" that presses your lower back into an exaggerated lumbar curve, or a headrest that pushes your head forward, will get you into trouble regardless of how "ergonomic" is it supposed to be or how expensive it is. So it's good to start with a chair that suits you and a good workspace setup.

The model workspace shown in the photos in this chapter has several aspects that are not ideal. For example, the seat of the chair is slanted backward, and the keyboard tray is placed on the desk, too high for optimum use. If this were my workspace, I would want a different chair and a pullout keyboard tray. (I now like to sit on a backless stool that is higher than a standard chair; this works well for me, now that I no longer need to work at a desk for hours at a time.) However, even if our employers provide good furniture for our workplaces, we must learn to deal with less than optimal seats and other furniture in many situations, including cars, public transportation, airplanes, doctors' waiting rooms, other people's houses, and so forth.

Even the perfect chair—if it existed—would not prevent you from slumping in it. I have seen people slump and tense their shoulders even using inflatable exercise balls and kneeling chairs, which supposedly "force" you to have good posture. And as we shall see in a later chapter, truly good posture is the opposite of forced: easy, natural, and free.

CHAPTER 4

Do You Really Know What You Are Doing? The Alexander Technique Skill of Awareness

In the previous chapter, I introduced Alexander's concept of "debauched kinesthesia," his delightfully Victorian term for the situation in which what a person believes he or she is doing, on the basis of his or her feeling sense, is inaccurate. As later chapters will show, there are a number of common beliefs about posture, breathing, and movement that will be unlearned through a course of Alexander Technique lessons. However, debauched kinesthesia is somewhat different: it involves not a conceptual mistake, but a mistaken interpretation of sensory information.

Habitual Postures and the Feeling Sense

Take a look at the photos "Before" and "After" on page 28, illustrating how a student who is a habitual slumper might look when he first comes for an Alexander Technique lesson, and then after his teacher has helped him to stand upright. As I explained in the previous chapter, it is very common in my teaching practice and that of every other Alexander Technique teacher I know for such a student to exclaim, when thus standing upright, "I feel like I am leaning backward." Indeed, in the second photo, this student is standing differently from his habitual way, and he accurately senses that his head and upper torso are further back in space than usual. So in a sense, the student's perception is correct: he is "leaning backward" relative to where he started. However, to the objective observer, he has gone from slumping forward to standing fully upright. Most people who go through this experience and then look at themselves in a mirror see that they are not in fact leaning backward and acknowledge that they are not actually doing what they thought they were doing on the basis of their feeling sense.

Before   After

Sometimes this insight is enough to result in a relatively quick change in a person's habitual stance. I have found this to be particularly true of people whose habit is to pull themselves upright in an effort to "stand up straight," as in the photo "Trying hard to stand up straight" on page 30. Unlike a slump, which at least feels like an easy thing to do, this posture involves a lot of work. It is usually not difficult for me to guide such a person to an easier upright stance, as in the photo "Easily upright." When I then show the student that what feels like slumping is actually quite upright, the response is often relief that one can have good posture with so little effort.

But change is not always so easy. If you habitually sit, stand, and walk with your shoulders slumped forward, your back in a big C-shaped curve, and the weight of your head out in front of your chest, your musculature will adapt to be sure that you don't fall forward. In particular, your neck and back muscles will work harder than they would otherwise need to work, lest the weight of your head cause you to topple forward and down. Your back muscles will become used to existing in a lengthened state and the muscles of the front of your body to existing in a shortened state. To further complicate matters, since the muscles in the back of your neck have to shorten in order to raise your head up so you can see in front of you, your neck muscles will be habitually tense and shortened.

The man in the photo "Slouching forward to work" on page 14 illustrates one version of this posture. If you usually sit this way, and then decide to "sit up straight," you will likely find it very hard work. Even if your concept of "good posture" is accurate—and for most people, it is not—sitting upright will require increased work in parts of you that are used to slacking off, and you are likely to be unable to maintain the new posture for very long.

Over time, people may lose the ability to come out of their habitual postures. Muscles that are always shortened eventually cannot lengthen fully. Muscles that are always slackened lose strength. Muscles that are always overworking become permanently tense. Fascial tissue tightens and becomes fixed within its habitual range of motion. This is why women who constantly wear high heels eventually find it uncomfortable to wear flats: their calf muscles have shortened and their entire bodies have adapted to sustain the particular balance required for heels. This is also why physical therapists typically address their patients' postural problems by having them stretch and strengthen different muscle groups.

However, even when the capacity to assume a different shape has not yet been lost, or has been regained through exercise and stretching, people tend to

Trying hard to stand
up straight

Easily upright

Slumping forward to work

revert to their habitual ways, especially when their attention is engaged with something other than posture. If you are used to standing in a slump, when you change your posture to stand more erect, all the muscles of your torso are taken out of their resting length: the muscles in the front of your body become longer than usual, and the muscles of your back shorter than usual. As a result, you feel a stretch in front and a shortening in back.

These sensations seem to be telling you that you are leaning backward. If you were really leaning backward, you would be in danger of falling, and would have to work to maintain your balance. So unless you are aware that your interpretation of what you are feeling is inaccurate, and have the skill to override your instinctive reactions, you will not sustain this new way of balancing. Instead, as soon as you get involved in working, socializing, or other demanding and interesting activities, you will revert to what you are used to doing, which feels normal and therefore "right." In short, you will go back to slumping.

I experienced all of these sensations and mistaken interpretations in my early lessons in the Alexander Technique. However, I had very little understanding of what was going on. It was a long time before I was able to separate the sensations from my interpretations. I was, in fact, a kinesthetic dunce. I had ignored and tuned out my feeling sense for a long time, and it took a long time for me to turn it back on and fine-tune it into something I could use to enhance my own well-being.

Proprioception and Kinesthesia

The "feeling sense," as I have been calling it, can also be called "kinesthesia" (as in Alexander's "debauched kinesthesia") and "proprioception." It is worth pausing to define these terms.

"Proprioception" comes from the physiological term "proprioceptor," a formation from the Latin *proprius* ("own") and the English *receptor*. The *Oxford English Dictionary* (second edition, Clarendon Press, 1989) (the "OED"), provides these definitions:

> **proprioceptor**. . . . Any sensory structure which receives stimuli arising within the tissues (other, usually, than the viscera), *esp.* one concerned with the sense of position and movement of a part of the body. . . .
>
> So "proprioception" is the reception of information by proprioceptors and its interpretation.

"Kinesthesia" (also "kinaesthesia," "kinaesthesis," and "kinesthesis") derives from the Greek words for "movement" and "sensation." Again from the OED:

> **kinaesthesis**. . . . The sense of muscular effort that accompanies a voluntary movement of the body. Also, the sense or faculty by which such sensations are perceived.

Thus, the two terms have similar meanings, and they are often used interchangeably. But regardless of which term is used, the sense they describe tells us the relationship of our different body parts to one another and to our environment, as well as the amount of work involved in any particular movement or posture.

We have nerves in our muscles and other tissues that communicate information to our brains about what is going on in those parts of us, and our brains interpret that information in light of our experiences. There may be several layers of interpretation, and we may not be consciously aware of all of them. To return to my example of the habitual slumper who stands upright for a change, the layers of interpretation might be as given below:

- This is different from the way I normally stand.
- My back muscles are working and my front muscles are being stretched.
- My weight has shifted from the front of my feet toward my heels.
- I'm leaning backward.
- I feel like I might fall.
- This feels wrong/weird/uncomfortable/unbalanced.
- This feels good and I wish I could maintain it.

The first statement is true, and the next two are probably factually correct as well. The fourth statement is not objectively true. The remainder are expressions of opinion.

In a typical first lesson in my teaching practice, a habitual slumper may articulate any or all of these interpretations, may come up with other interpretations, or may say nothing at all. But without exception, sooner or later, my students revert to habit. This may occur a few moments after their experience of standing more upright, as soon as they walk out of my office, or a few days after their lesson. It requires time for students to learn to stand and sit differently often enough, and for long enough periods, for their bodies to adapt to the new way of being, so that it starts to feel normal, natural, and right. Various changes happen during this period. The length and tone of the student's muscles shift.

Some muscles adapt to a longer resting length, others to a shorter. Some muscles begin to be more relaxed when they are not actively working. Others may have increased resting tone. Some may become stronger because they are being used more consistently in daily activity. And throughout the process, the student's interpretation of the various muscle sensations gradually changes as well.

The period of time required for these changes to happen may vary from a few weeks to a few months. But I believe everyone, regardless of age or condition, is capable of making them, if the student is motivated enough, and the teacher's way of working is congenial and interesting enough, for the student to persevere. Each person's body is different. Permanent structural changes may occur as a result of age, injury, or disease. I don't aim to get every student to have the same shape, and I do not presume to know exactly what outward changes will be possible. But regardless of body type and limitations, all of us can learn to make better use of the bodies we have.

Whenever I am tempted to assume that someone's current shape is fixed and incapable of changing, I remember a woman who began lessons with me in her mid-70s because she was experiencing back pain. She told me in her first lesson that she did not like the way she was getting hunched over as she aged. I soon realized that this was not a matter of tissues that were frozen in this shape. In her first lesson, I spent about 20 minutes working with her as she lay on her back on my teaching table, and at the end of that time, the forward curve of her back had decreased significantly. Over the course of a number of months, she took weekly lessons and gave her diligent attention to what she was learning as she walked, stretched, and worked out between lessons. The result was a dramatic change in her posture, with her previously bent-over back becoming quite upright. She also reported having less back pain in her daily activities.

Why Does the Feeling Sense Go Wrong?

All of the interpretations listed above arise out of the contrast between what the slumper normally feels and the different sensations associated with standing more upright. The contrast itself can be illuminating: standing differently for a few moments can tell a person a great deal about his or her normal way of standing. This is because, when it comes to the feeling sense, what is habitual fades into the background of our attention and ceases to be perceived, unless there is a good reason for it to come to the foreground again.

I often tell my students that in our lessons, we pay close attention to things of which, in our everyday lives, we are entirely unconscious—and rightly so.

If we had to pay attention to each bodily sensation and movement every moment of the day, we would never be able to do anything else. In Alexander Technique lessons, however, we hone the ability to tune in to this normally submerged information when doing so is helpful. Doing simple movements in a nonhabitual way is one strategy for discovering our habits. Alexander "chair work"—sitting, standing up, and sitting down again—is commonly used to cultivate this awareness and explore habits of movement and posture.

To get a sense of this, consider the question of what you do with your neck when you move from sitting and standing. Perhaps you are thinking, "not much." Don't be so sure! Or perhaps you are just realizing that you have no idea, even though logically the neck would not seem to have much to do in this activity. So find out, using this simple exercise:

- Sit in a chair from which you can easily stand up (e.g., a desk chair or a dining chair, rather than an overstuffed easy chair).
- Place one hand on the back of your neck.
- Stand up and sit down several times, feeling what happens in the neck muscles under your hand.

If you find it difficult to feel anything under your hand, position your chair so that you have a three-quarter view of yourself in a mirror, and watch what happens to your head in relationship to your body as you get up and down, or ask someone else to observe you and report.

This activity is often used by Alexander Technique teachers to introduce students to the concept of the "primary control," which I discussed in Chapter 1. If you were able to observe anything as you stood up and sat down again, you probably noticed the muscles of your neck tightening each time. If you didn't feel this with your hand, you might still have observed in the mirror that the distance between the back of your head and your back got shorter, showing that the muscles in the back of your neck contracted to bring the back of your head closer to your shoulders and back. And if you are like most people, until I brought this to your attention, you had no idea that you did this.

In itself, this head movement, though unnecessary for sitting down and standing up, may not seem particularly wrong or important. However, it is evidence of a larger pattern, a habit that most people have, of contracting the neck muscles in order to do almost any activity. In essence, we tend to react to any stimulus with a miniature version of what we do in reaction to a genuine threat: a small, subtle version of the startle response described in Chapter 3. When you start observing this in yourself and others, you'll find it everywhere: talking heads on TV bob forward and back to emphasize every other word; drivers push their faces forward over the steering wheel; teenagers hunch over their video-games; businesspeople contract the back of their necks as they press their eyes close to their smartphones and type frantically with their thumbs.

Alexander did the same thing when he went on stage to recite. He called it "pulling the head back and down" and described its opposite—what happened when he allowed his neck "to be free" as "allowing the head to move forward and up." This terminology can be quite confusing. One way to understand it is to observe the space between the back of the head and the back of the neck. If the neck muscles tighten, as in the startle response, the space between them shortens. Compare the two photos "Pulling the head back and down" and "Allowing the head to move forward and up" on pages 37 and 38. In the first photo, the man's back is curved forward, so he has to crane his neck in order to look straight ahead at his computer screen. Alexander would say that he is pulling his head "back and down"—not in space, but in relationship to his back. In the second photo, he sits upright, so he can look straight ahead without craning his neck: his neck is "free" (not overworking) so that his head can move "forward and up"—again, in relationship to his back.

Consider when you might pull your own head back and down without realizing it: perhaps when you are called upon to speak in a meeting or in court, when you are frantically writing a complex document that is due by the end of the day, or when you hear the chime of an e-mail arriving while trying to have a relaxing dinner with family or friends. This is what I did when I used to tense my neck every time the phone in my office rang. But it was habitual—so I never noticed it until it started to hurt. It's not optimal to tighten your neck muscles with every move and in every situation that requires a response, and with repetition it can lead to all sorts of problems. So why didn't I notice it and correct the problem before it got out of hand?

First of all, I had no training in how my body is supposed to work and how to best coordinate it. Had I been a trained dancer or athlete, I would have had some ideas about this (though they might have been wrong ideas, as I will explain later). But I was an academic sort, interested in mental rather than physical pursuits and accomplishments. I just assumed that I would always have the physical capacity to engage in the reading, writing, analysis, discussion, and negotiation that were part of my job as a lawyer. I knew I should exercise to maintain my health, and I even did so sometimes. But it never occurred to me that I needed to think about movement and my body while I was working at my job.

Pulling the head back and down

Allowing the head to move forward and up

And once this idea was forced upon my consciousness by pain, I still thought that it was impossible to do both at once, to think about my physical self while engaged in the intellectually demanding practice of law.

So I started with an underdeveloped feeling sense. And then pain set in, paradoxically deadening my feeling sense even further. When we are in acute pain, as from an injury, our muscles tense up around the part that hurts to protect it, in a phenomenon referred to as "splinting." If you have ever had your back "go out," you have experienced this. Generally, what happens when your back "goes out" is that you sprain your back in one sudden movement, or through repetitive strain, and the muscles of your back contract to protect the injured area.

Splinting can be a helpful response to acute injury and pain, but in the long run, it can create problems. For injury to heal, blood must circulate to the injured area, but muscle tension reduces blood flow. And splinting sometimes continues even after the injury has healed. This muscle tension can itself cause pain, which reinforces the tension, which causes more pain—truly a vicious circle. The tension also interferes with the proprioceptors in the injured area. Again, this makes sense as a short-term response to acute injury, when it deadens pain. But if the tension remains, the feeling sense continues to be deadened.

This happened to my neck. I was in a great deal of pain for much of the time over a period of several years. As a result, I ceased to be able to feel much of anything in my neck, other than the pain. When I first began to take Alexander Technique lessons, I was hindered by this lack of sensation: I literally could not feel the difference when my teacher helped me make subtle changes in the way my head balanced on top of my spine.

So the feeling sense can go wrong for a number of reasons and in a number of ways:

- If you always sit, stand, and move in the same way, that way will feel normal and might even be below the level of your consciousness.
- If you don't generally pay attention to what you are feeling, you may cease to feel it.
- If you are in pain, your body's reaction to the pain may deaden your feeling sense.
- If you think of the mind and the body as separate phenomena, you may not be aware of your body when you are in "mental" mode.

In the following chapters, we will examine how the Alexander Technique uses the skill of awareness to reawaken, enhance, and re-educate the feeling sense.

CHAPTER 5

What Is Good Posture?

Most people have some idea of what good posture is supposed to look like. This idea is generally at odds with what an Alexander Technique teacher considers good posture. Furthermore, the way people go about attaining this good posture is very different from the approach taken in Alexander Technique lessons.

Ever since I began to try to explain to people what the Alexander Technique was all about, I have observed very interesting reactions. Almost without exception, when they realize that the technique might have something to do with posture, they begin to fidget self-consciously and contort themselves in various ways. The individual variations on the before-and-after positions are endless, but the general idea is the same: as soon as they think of the concept of posture, they begin to realign their body parts into something resembling what they think is good posture. Of course, soon enough, they let it go and revert to their habitual posture.

Many Alexander Technique teachers don't like to even mention the word "posture." They think the very word has so many wrong connotations that it should be avoided. I think this reticence is unnecessary. I take the Humpty Dumptian point of view: the important thing is not what people think a word might mean, but what we say it means. ("'When I use a word,' Humpty Dumpty said, in rather a scornful tone, 'it means just what I choose it to mean—neither more nor less.'" *Through the Looking Glass*, Lewis Carroll.) Thus, I prefer to confront the issue by stating frankly that the Alexander Technique does involve posture, but that it defines "good posture" and how to achieve it in a very different way than most approaches.

Probably everyone has been scolded, at one time or another, to "sit up straight!" Perhaps at some point in life you internalized that admonition and began periodically to tell yourself to stop slouching. The usual way of carrying out such an order involves using the muscles to push and pull body parts into new positions: the chest is pulled up, the shoulder blades are pressed back and down, the pelvis is tilted this way or tucked that way, and so forth. Some people do this as if imitating a soldier coming to attention. Others seem to have in mind the image of a dancer on stage. Either way, they contract their muscles to pull their body into a particular position and hold it there. It tends to be very stiffening. And it's hard work.

There's no doubt that bad posture is hard on the body. But Alexander Technique teachers believe that what most people consider to be good posture is equally hard on the body. For one thing, it restricts breathing significantly. You can test this proposition for yourself by assuming a good military posture and walking around, paying attention to your breath as you do so. Then let go of that posture, and see what happens to your breath.

Another reason what most people think of as good posture is not so good is that it is generally maintained by using excessive muscle tension in the neck, shoulders, and back, which in turn stiffens the limbs as well. If you habitually slouch in your chair, you probably can notice the amount of extra work that is required to "sit up straight" according to the usual idea. On the other hand, people who habitually maintain what they have been taught to believe is good posture often don't realize how much they are overworking. They have learned to carry themselves stiffly erect either as children, from relatives or teachers, or as adults, from physical therapists, dance teachers, or yoga instructors. Those who taught them to do this had the best of intentions, but the result is inflexibility, impairment of full breathing, and even pain: ironically, the same problems that can result from slouching.

In my teaching practice, several lawyers have come for lessons with what most people would say looked like good posture, but who had suffered for years from mysterious neck and back pain that could not be traced to any injury or disease. It was immediately apparent to me, with my Alexander Technique lens, that each of them was holding his or her back and neck ramrod straight, with very tense muscles. As we worked together on letting go of that tension, these students were able to experience being fully upright with much less effort, and the pain gradually disappeared.

Posture, Breathing, and Voice

Breathing is largely an autonomic function, continuing night and day, as long as you are alive. You can stop your breathing by holding your breath, but at a certain point you will either have to begin again or lose consciousness—at which point you will resume breathing. You can also do things, consciously or not, that interfere with free, efficient breathing. Two examples that I have already introduced are slouching and "standing up straight."

Both of these habits interfere with breathing by restricting movement in your torso. Slouching involves collapsing, putting downward pressure on your torso, especially the front of the chest. Stereotypical "good posture" involves contracting muscles in the back and shoulders and holding them tight.

When you breathe freely, your entire torso moves. The prime movers of the breath are the diaphragm and the ribs. Your diaphragm is a large muscle that bisects your torso. Your ribs envelop the top half of your body, beginning above the collar bone. Within the ribcage are your lungs and heart; all your other organs lie below the diaphragm.

With each inhalation, the diaphragm descends, the ribs expand up and out, and air flows into your lungs. With each exhalation, the diaphragm ascends, the ribs release down and in, and the air flows out of your lungs. These movements of your torso are three-dimensional: your back, sides, and front all move with your breathing.

In addition, when the diaphragm descends with an inhalation, the internal organs that are housed below the diaphragm are displaced. This is why your belly moves when you breathe. You may have heard the instruction to "breathe from your diaphragm" or "breathe into your belly." I believe the intention of such instructions is to encourage you to allow for this movement in the lower part of your torso and to discourage raising the shoulders and upper chest with each inhalation. Unfortunately, many people seem to respond by actively preventing movement in the upper part of the torso, holding their shoulders and sternums rigid. As we have seen, the common idea of good posture also tends to involve tightening muscles of the shoulders, chest, and back in an effort to stand up straight ("pull your shoulders back and down, tuck your chin, raise your chest up!").

Whatever the motivation, however, holding the shoulders, chest, and back tight significantly limits the range of motion of the upper ribs, which lie underneath the collarbone, sternum, and shoulder blades. Since the ribcage works as a unit, this restricts the movement of the lower ribs as well. Slouching also restricts movement of the ribs by putting downward pressure on the whole torso. Restricted movement in the ribs means restricted movement of air in and out of the lungs. Thus, posture and breathing are intimately related.

Many people have the idea that to breathe well, they should first "take a deep breath." They may also engage in practices such as manipulating their ribs to control their breathing or attempting to make their inhalations and exhalations a specific, consistent length. I will not comment here on the value of such practices for particular activities such as yoga, meditation, or singing. I will say that they have no place in everyday activities. A healthy human being is quite capable of breathing fully and freely, without any manipulation at all, if he or she stops interfering with the natural mechanisms. And the way to start is not by taking a deep breath, but by letting the breath out, and then allowing a new breath to come in.

When Alexander Technique students learn to sit and stand upright without undue effort, their breathing improves as a natural consequence. The improvement can also be heard in their voices. Speaking and singing are done with an exhalation. The quality, stamina, and strength of the voice improve with freer, fuller breathing. This is one reason actors and singers frequently study the Alexander Technique.

I maintain that lawyers, too, are performers who can be more effective with good vocal production. When you speak in court, negotiate a contract, or counsel a client, you seek to persuade and inspire confidence, and your auditors respond, consciously or unconsciously, to the tone of your voice. If you sound tired, raspy, squeaky, short of breath, too soft, too loud, or otherwise unpleasant or harassed, you are less effective. But if you manipulate your voice to try to be more effective, you risk damaging it by excess effort. This can happen, for example, when a woman deliberately speaks at a lower pitch than is natural to her voice. People do tend, unfortunately, to consider lower-pitched (i.e., male) voices as more authoritative. However, over the long term, overriding one's natural voice can lead to strain and fatigue.

The next time you find yourself in a boring meeting with long-winded speakers, take the opportunity to observe and listen. Consider the speakers' posture and movement. Do they look rigid, collapsed, or upright? Are they standing or sitting very still, or do they move a bit? Are their gestures fluid or jerky? Do they seem listless, calm, energetic, or frenzied? Then listen to their voices. Are they pleasant or unpleasant in quality? Is it easy to follow what they are saying? Do the voices express any particular emotion—eagerness, anger, anxiety, humor, hostility, or enjoyment? Do the voices elicit any visceral reaction in you? Can you make any connection between what you see in a particular speaker's posture and movement and the vocal quality that you hear, the emotional connotation of the voice, or the reaction it evokes in you? When it is your turn to speak, observe your own posture and movement and listen to the sound of your own voice with the same questions in mind.

The actor's skill of being heard on stage without amplification is commonly referred to as "projecting" or "throwing" the voice, as if the voice were a physical object that could be moved through space as you might throw a baseball. If you think about what you know about sound, you will probably realize that this image is misleading. When we hear sound, we are perceiving vibrations that travel through air and other substances. When I speak, the air exhaled from my lungs crosses my vocal folds ("voice box") and through my mouth. My vocal folds vibrate, creating sound waves that are amplified and shaped by my body, including the cavities in my head. Those sound waves travel through the air to your ear, where they cause movement of the eardrum and other structures, conveying information to your brain that you experience as hearing the sound of my voice.

Now think of what you do when you want to increase the volume and strength of your voice. Does it involve forcing the air out of your lungs by tightening the muscles of your torso? Do you tense up your neck, jaw, and face? This is actually counterproductive. If you have ever played a musical instrument, you know that the sound is muted if you stop the instrument from vibrating. Even if you haven't ever touched an instrument, you probably have struck a wineglass to make it chime and stopped the sound by taking hold of the rim. Similarly, to make your voice more resonant and audible, you must allow free vibration in your body, not clamp down on it.

The ease and freedom of movement that you can learn in Alexander Technique lessons thus can contribute both to freer breathing and to better vocal production by enabling you to let go of tension patterns that restrict your breath and dampen the resonance of your voice. When your breathing is not strained and your voice resonates freely without excess effort, you can choose your volume, pacing, and tone in response to the circumstances: you can speak softly and be heard in a quiet office; you can speak loudly and be heard in a noisy conference room; you can speak clearly in an overly reverberant courtroom; you can even speak quietly enough to use a microphone effectively. You can also allow your message to influence the tone of your voice and slow down or speed up the pace of your words to make your point intelligible and engaging.

The Most Basic Skill: Balancing Your Own Head

As we have seen, Alexander first developed his technique in order to overcome chronic vocal fatigue when performing as an actor. When he began to teach others, he became known as "The Breathing Man" because of the improvements in respiration that his students enjoyed. The key to the improvements in his own voice and in the breathing of his students was an improved balance of the head on top of the spine.

To discover how to sit and stand upright easily, without slouching and without excess muscle work, you must relearn how to balance your head easily at the top of your spine. The human head sits atop the spine at the atlanto-occipital joint, formed where two shallow indentations in the occipital bone of the skull (the occipital condyles) meet the atlas, the top vertebra of the spinal column. You can get a sense of where this joint is by placing your fingers gently in your ears and imagining a line connecting your fingertips: at the center of this line is your atlanto-occipital joint. Note how deep inside you this place is: you can't touch it directly, as it is several inches in front of the back of your neck and skull, and it is at the level of the roof of your mouth.

If you nod your head, as if to say "yes," by moving your head without bending your neck, you will be moving on your atlanto-occipital joint. Notice that this is different from the movements you can make by moving at lower points along your neck or by pushing your head forward in space. The nod on your atlanto-occipital joint is a rocking movement that allows your head to rotate in a range of about 40 degrees around its center.

So your skull balances on a small, shallow joint deep within your head. One image sometimes used to illustrate this is a seal balancing a ball on its snout: the ball is the head, and the snout is the atlanto-occipital joint. But this image is misleading in one respect. In order for the seal to balance the ball, it must keep the center of gravity of the ball directly over its snout. But when the human head is well balanced, its center of gravity is above and in front of the atlanto-occipital joint. This is possible because, unlike the ball on the seal's snout, the human head need not balance unaided by anything but its contact with the atlas; rather, the muscles of the neck and torso engage to keep the head from falling forward. If you have ever fallen asleep while seated upright, you know that this is so: when you go to sleep, your neck muscles slacken and, if you are not reclining, your head tends to fall forward and down toward your chest.

When everything is going well, this system of support for the head works extremely well. When your neck and back muscles provide just the tone needed to support the head's balance on the atlas, no more and no less, your head balances easily and is free to move on the atlanto-occipital joint as needed for you to see and hear your environment. Its weight also puts a gentle upward stretch on the supporting muscles of your back and neck, helping your spine to stay long and flexible. You could imagine your head, neck, and back as a pulley system, with a weight hanging down the front part of the pulley causing the rope to be pulled up in back.

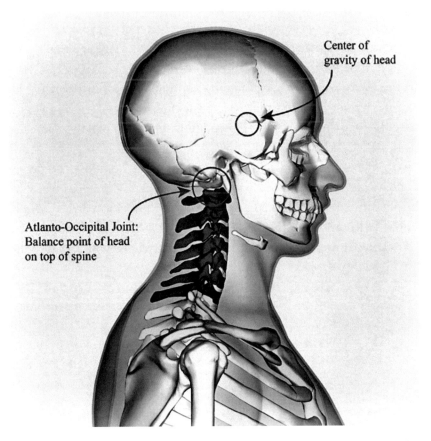

Center of
gravity of head

Atlanto-Occipital Joint:
Balance point of head
on top of spine

The atlanto-occipital joint and the center of gravity of the head

When the head is out of balance, however, trouble ensues. The habits we have looked at in earlier chapters all have a tendency to interfere with the efficient balance of the weight of the head. Usually this involves contracting the muscles of the neck, as in the startle reflex described in Chapter 3. Two other ways in which we tend to overwork our necks in real life are shown in the photos "Slumping forward to work" and "Pulling the head back to see ahead."

Can you see, in each photo, where the center of gravity the head is in relationship to the neck and back? You can almost see the weight of the skull pulling and pressing down on the spine and torso. If you sit, stand, and move in this way, instead of allowing the weight of your head to lengthen your spine, you are actively, albeit unconsciously, using it to compress your spine. This compression detracts from the flexibility and resilience of your spinal column and hence of your entire torso, limiting your breathing and impairing your balance. The accompanying tension in your limbs restricts their mobility. The extra work done by your entire body to remain upright and move about despite these imbalances and rigidities leads to fatigue and pain.

So from an Alexander Technique standpoint, the point of good posture is not to align your body parts in a particular way and hold them in place, but to tap into an easier, more balanced way to manage the weight of your own head, allowing your whole body to expand into resilience—to be both strong and flexible. The skill that Alexander called "direction" is used to evoke this response.

Slumping forward to work

Pulling the head back to see ahead

CHAPTER 6

Achieve More by Doing Less (The Alexander Technique Skill of Direction)

At my very first lesson with my first Alexander Technique teacher, I learned to do what she called "constructive rest" and began to practice it at least once daily. At the time, I was on disability leave, devoting all my attention to getting better, so I had plenty of time to try out anything that might help. After I returned to work, I continued this practice. I sometimes would do constructive rest in the morning before going to work or just before going to bed.

But most often, I chose to do it in the late afternoon, in my office. I would tell my secretary to hold my calls; place a "do not disturb" sign on the door to my office and close it; and then lie down on my back on the floor, with my lower legs resting on the seat of my desk chair, and my head resting on Peter Romeo's book about Rule 16b-3. (That book was quite useful in my practice, but it also happened to be just the right thickness for this activity.) And there I would stay for 10 to 15 minutes, just lying on the floor doing nothing. I invariably arose refreshed and energized for more work.

What Is Constructive Rest?

Constructive rest, also known in the Alexander Technique community as "lying-down work," "having a lie-down," "semi-supine," and "active rest," is a practice of lying down on a firm surface for a brief period, typically 10 to 20 minutes. A portion of most private Alexander Technique lessons is spent in "table work," with the student lying on his or her back on a table while the teacher helps him or her quiet down, let go of muscle tension, expand in all directions, and practice thinking the Alexander directions (about which I will say more later in this chapter). Constructive rest is the self-help version of table work.

Like most Alexander Technique teachers, I tell my students that their homework is to do constructive rest every day between lessons. In fact, I tell everyone who comes for a first lesson that if they learn only one thing, I hope it will be to cultivate the habit of constructive rest.

The key elements of constructive rest are as follows:

- Lie on your back on a firm surface, not a soft one. A rug, blanket, or exercise mat on the floor is ideal. A couch or bed is not. While you might not be comfortable sleeping on the floor, most people have no trouble lying down on the floor for a brief period. The firmness actually helps your muscles release better than when you are on a softer surface. If you have difficulty getting down onto the floor or back up again, your Alexander Technique teacher can help you work out easier ways to do so.

- Support your head on a short stack of paperback books or magazines, so that your head neither falls backward nor protrudes upward. Your head should be in the same relationship to your torso as if you were standing upright and your head were balancing easily at the top of your spine.

- It is preferable not to lie with both legs fully extended, as it tends to put a strain on the lower back. Place one or both feet on the floor with bended knee(s) or support your lower legs on the seat of a chair.

- While you remain on the floor, see if you can quiet down your thoughts. Notice the contact of your body with the floor. Observe your breathing. Think of allowing your muscles to release, so that your body can expand in all directions.

- After you have quieted down and begun to notice the effects of constructive rest, you might begin to think the Alexander directions to yourself. A version of these directions appears in Chapter 3 at page 22.

- After a time, you may need to adjust the height of the books on which your head rests, or move your limbs or torso to allow for the extra length and width that develops as you remain on the floor. In an Alexander Technique lesson, your teacher will do these things for you and show you how you can do them on your own.

Why Do Constructive Rest?

Constructive rest is a great way to rest your back, to refresh yourself after too much sitting, and to calm down when you have been overstressed. Even if you don't take Alexander Technique lessons, and even if you don't really think about anything while you lie on the floor, the simple act of allowing your entire body

Constructive rest with knees bent

Constructive rest with lower legs on chair seat

Too many books

Head falling backward

Good head support

to be fully supported while doing nothing is restorative. As long as you feel comfortable in the position you have set up for yourself, you really can't do it wrong, because there's nothing to do.

If you add to the experience thinking the Alexander directions to yourself—in essence, thinking about expanding in all directions—you'll enhance the benefits by clarifying for yourself what sort of changes you would like to bring about as you rest. And if you are taking Alexander Technique lessons, constructive rest will reinforce the work you do with your teacher and allow you to revisit that wonderful state of calm energy and expansion that you get from your time on your teacher's table.

Some people quickly become fans of this practice. I have noticed, however, that a significant number of my students resist it strenuously. They have various reasons for not taking my advice. Sometimes the problems are practical: it's cold on their floor, they have difficulty getting down and up again, or their cat walks all over them. But more often, they tell me they simply don't have time to "do nothing."

It certainly seems to be the case that most lawyers and other professionals spend so many hours on things they are obligated to do for their jobs and their families that they have little time for self-care, even for things as vital as getting enough sleep and exercise. In this light, I can see that taking even 10 minutes for yet another obligation seems impossible, especially if you think of that obligation as requiring you to "do nothing."

For me, though constructive rest is not doing nothing, any more than eating nourishing food and getting sufficient sleep are doing nothing (to name two other activities that busy lawyers often neglect). It is a healthy practice that restores and supports me for further productive activity. I think the problem lies in our society's concept of what it means to "do" something.

Doing, Thinking, and Doing Nothing

Direction, in the Alexander Technique, refers to instructions given to oneself, that is, thoughts about how to respond to the stimulus to do something: how to move or how to be still. In the simplest sense, direction means telling yourself to undo the startle response. I have set forth one verbal formulation of this idea in Chapter 3. The first step is to stop overworking the neck muscles—or rather, to conceive a desire to stop overworking them. Alexander's phrase is "I allow my neck to be free" (free of overwork, that is). When some of that overwork stops, the head rotates a bit up and over the atlanto-occipital joint, rebalancing the weight of the head so that the center of gravity of the head is restored to its natural place above and in front of the atlanto-occipital joint ("to allow my head to go forward and up"). The weight of the head then helps the spine decompress a bit, and the whole torso expands in response ("to allow my whole torso to lengthen and widen"). This expansion of the torso in turn stimulates an undoing of the contraction of the arms and legs into the torso ("to allow my knees to release forward and away and my heels to release back and down"). As the whole body expands, it becomes lighter, more balanced, freer to move, and more energized. While we of necessity talk about the directions as a series of steps, in fact when they are working at their best, the changes happen all at once, in response to a simple thought.

It's easy to misconceive or misexecute these directions. As we have seen, the Alexander Technique skill of inhibition is literally "nondoing"—pausing before responding to a stimulus, long enough to consider whether and how to react. Directing is also not doing something, at least not in the way most of us experience "doing." No deliberate muscle action is involved. It's like what happens when you make a tight fist and then simply stop tensing your hand: the shape of your fist changes, even though you have not purposely moved anything. In the same way, when I think about allowing my neck to be free, I may notice my muscles responding to my thoughts, but my primary attention is given to sending the thought, not to trying to do or feel something. The thought has an effect because I have practiced the thinking and experienced the desired change repeatedly, honing my skill and strengthening the association between the thought and the bodily state that it describes.

When I introduce new students to the concept that just thinking something could change one's physical state, I am often met with a certain amount of incomprehension and disbelief. The idea that one can improve one's posture just by thinking is certainly not a common one. So I like to use a variant of the game of "Simon Says" to help people begin to notice how their bodies respond to thoughts. You can try this out yourself with the help of another person or a small group. One person plays the role of leader, who gives simple orders to the others to do things like raise a hand, stand up, turn around, and so forth.

The game has three rounds. In round 1, the participants are instructed to do exactly what the leader tells them to do. In round 2, the participants are told to refrain from doing what the leader tells them to do—to just sit there and do nothing. In the final round, participants are given three choices: to obey, to do nothing, or to do something different. For example, if the leader says to raise your right hand, you might choose to raise your right hand, to remain motionless, or to raise your left hand. Participants are asked, in this third round, to endeavor to make the decision how to react only after they hear the order, rather than planning ahead.

In most groups, in round 2, there are several people who discover themselves reflexively following orders, even though they are supposed to do nothing. Even those who do not leap into action usually notice a small reaction in their muscles: if the order is to raise the right hand, the muscles of the right arm contract as soon as the words are spoken, as if to initiate the movement. And in round 3, it is very interesting to watch people discover that it can be quite challenging not to decide in advance which of the three choices to make in response to the next order.

This game exposes my students to the concept of inhibition because it asks them to refrain from responding to a stimulus long enough to remember whether they are supposed to be following the order or not, and, in round 3, long enough to first hear the next order and then make a fresh choice about what to do in response to it. It also provides a clear experience of how quickly and automatically the body reacts to the stimulus of a thought. In the case of the game, the thought comes from the outside in the form of a simple order given by the leader, with the overlay of the ground rules of the game and the thoughts the process stimulates in the participants. In the case of Alexander's directions—which, as it happens, he also sometimes referred to as "orders"—the thoughts come from within. As we have seen, unlike in the game, the Alexander directions are not randomly chosen, but specifically designed to evoke a whole-body response of improved coordination, balance, and muscle tone.

Here we reach the point at which I find words become truly inadequate. I can show you pictures of what Alexander Technique teachers call "good use of the self" (our jargon for good posture and movement), and you can imitate them. I can refer you back to the version of Alexander's "directions" that I set forth in Chapter 3. I could describe ways for you, on your own, to continue exploring your own head balance and discovering the benefits of improving it. But the truth is, there is no way I can guarantee that any of these different ways of explaining the skill of direction will enable you to experience it on your own. And there is a reasonably good chance that if you try to carry out the directions on your own, you'll end up stiff or tense and maybe even aggravate your usual aches and pains.

On the other hand, if you take Alexander Technique lessons, your teacher will use both words and touch, as well as his or her own skills of awareness, inhibition, and direction, to help you experience how a few clear, simple thoughts can change your body. This sounds almost mystical, and sometimes it does feel like magic. But I know from experience that it is a real phenomenon and a real skill that anyone can learn with attention and practice.

CHAPTER 7

Further Learning

By now it should be clear that the Alexander Technique is considered by its adherents to be a form of education. It is often described as "kinesthetic re-education." The Alexander Technique undoubtedly can have therapeutic effects, and from the beginning, many have sought it out to address problems with their physical or mental health. However, Alexander referred to the clients who sought his help as "pupils" and to the sessions they had with him as "lessons." And today, those who carry on his work generally identify themselves as teachers with students, not therapists or practitioners with patients or clients.

It should also be clear that reading about the concepts of the technique is no substitute for in-person instruction from a qualified teacher. To give meaning to the words and concepts described above, Alexander Technique teachers use their hands to help their students let go of unnecessary muscle tension, generate appropriate muscle tone, and redirect their energy more efficiently, to move, sit, and stand while allowing for a lengthening spine and an easy head balance. Through repetition, the words and images we use to express this "better use of ourselves" become linked to the experiences, and the student gradually learns to use awareness, inhibition, and direction in everyday life, without the teacher's help.

Teaching Models

There are two main models of teaching the Alexander Technique: individual private lessons and group classes. Individual private lessons typically last between 30 minutes and an hour, during which the teacher gives a great deal of hands-on guidance to the student in movement. Usually, the student spends a portion of the lesson resting on a massage-type table while the teacher uses his or her hands to help the student release excess tension, quiet the nervous system, and practice awareness, inhibition, and direction. Group classes range from a few students to very large groups, led by one teacher with or without help from other teachers. Both models have benefits and detriments. In my opinion, individual private lessons are preferable for people with significant pain or disability, who usually require more individual attention and hands-on help from a teacher than is possible with a group. On the other hand, group classes are generally less expensive, and some people prefer a group learning experience.

Whether we teach individuals or groups, the educational framework is important to Alexander Technique teachers. There are aspects of the technique, particularly in private lessons, that may seem to resemble relaxation therapy or massage, but we place great emphasis on engaging our students' active thinking and attention in the process. For example, most teachers will remind their students not to close their eyes and "zone out" during table work. We want our students to expect to learn something that they will put into practice in their daily lives, when they are alert and engaged with the world.

How Long Will It Take?

Many people naturally want to get some idea of how long they will have to take lessons or classes in order to have learned the Alexander Technique. The only honest answer to this is, "it depends. . . ."

In an earlier chapter, I said that learning the Alexander Technique is like learning a foreign language. This is a good way to think about the question of how long it will take. It depends on what you want to achieve and how adept a learner you turn out to be.

If you are good at learning foreign languages, and your goal is merely to be able to say and understand a few phrases in Italian before your trip to Italy, I think we could safely predict that an hour with an instructor or a language tape will be more than sufficient. If you are not good at learning foreign languages, or your goal is to read Dante's *Divine Comedy* in the original, you can expect that it will take much longer.

What I always tell prospective students who ask me this is that if they take one private lesson with me, they will leave with sufficient insight into what is involved to decide if it's worth investing some more time and money in learning the technique. After that, it's very hard to predict: some people find that they get what they need in ten lessons or fewer; some continue for many months; still others discover that they want to continue indefinitely, either as a way to maintain what they have learned or because they find that they continue to enjoy the process of learning and improving their skills.

What's Next?

I hope that by now, you are eager to experience the Alexander Technique for yourself, by working with a certified teacher. Appendix 2 provides information about teacher certification standards and how to find a teacher in your area.

When you go for lessons or a class, prepare yourself to experience something entirely new. From the beginning of my study of the Alexander Technique, I realized this was nothing like the academic learning at which I had been so successful. I knew how to ace an exam, but I didn't know how to "allow my neck to be free," as my teacher kept asking. And I certainly didn't understand what she meant when she told me that I shouldn't "do" anything at all.

At first, the idea that I could deliberately use my thinking to profoundly affect my body was entirely alien. I kept going to lessons not because I accepted this premise, but because after 45 minutes with my teacher, I always felt better: lighter, taller, easier in my body. I attributed this entirely to my teacher's skill: her touch seemed to transform me in a way I could not understand. In fact, it was like magic. I told my friends that having an Alexander Technique lesson was like getting a full-body massage, except that the teacher was barely touching me.

I recall my early lessons as a sort of trickle-down learning. It was as if the new way of being was insinuating itself into me, even though I did not understand it. And then I began to notice that I could bring some of this about myself, by using the skills that my teacher had been teaching me and, equally important, modeling in herself. I became more and more interested in trying my new skills on my own, between lessons. At first, I was most successful at this when I was doing something that did not require much cognitive engagement, like walking. When I turned to reading, writing, or talking, I found it difficult to keep any attention on what I was doing with my body.

This, too, was a habit: a habit of conceiving of mind and body as separate, and of considering mental activity and physical activity as mutually exclusive. When I was in lawyer mode, reading, talking, analyzing—in other words, "thinking" as I understood the word—I paid no attention to my physicality. The reverse was also true; I was not good at thinking while moving.

Of course, people who work at a high level of physical skill, like dancers and athletes, think about what they are doing as they do it. However, somehow

I had gotten the idea that they could do this because they were physically gifted, and I could not because I was not a natural athlete. Until I began lessons in the Alexander Technique, it never occurred to me that this was a skill I could develop and use. I'm still no dancer or athlete, but now, when I swim, hike, or engage in other physical activities that I enjoy, I am able to think about what I am doing as I do it. And as I write these words, I am able to be aware of and give some attention to my body—the only form of multitasking that I think is actually productive and healthy.

The Alexander Technique and the Legal Profession

People who hear about my midlife change of profession sometimes ask whether my legal career was worth it, considering the health problems it caused me, or whether, if I had it to do all over again, I would choose to practice law. I find these questions impossible to answer. My twenty-five years as a lawyer are too much a part of who I am today to imagine my life had I chosen a different path.

I am also frequently asked if I miss being a lawyer. The truth is, I do not. I gained many valuable skills and made many good friends in those years. There were aspects of my legal career that were enjoyable at the time. On balance, however, I am much happier and healthier now that I have more time to take care of myself. I don't know if I could go back to working as I did before, and I have no intention of finding out.

These unanswerable questions about my past choices lead me to wonder whether there could be a middle way—if not for me, then for others. I know of many lawyers at various stages in their careers who are striving to find it: a way of doing high-quality, interesting work as a lawyer and making a good living, while still getting enough sleep and exercise and having some time for family, friends, and leisure activities. This kind of balance is not easy to find, especially in the world of major law firms. And perhaps that is inevitable: to engage in any occupation at the highest levels generally requires that one's time, energy, and attention be largely devoted to that occupation. When I worked at a big law firm, I accepted the conditions and considered it my own responsibility to leave when I could no longer cope with them.

But does it follow that the work environment at law firms cannot be improved? Let us accept, for purposes of discussion, the premise that lawyers must make their work their highest priority during their prime working years and spend most of their waking hours working. Does it follow that they must be as exhausted, anxious, stressed out, and miserable as so many of them are?

Let's imagine a process by which this state of things might begin to change, using the concepts and skills of the Alexander Technique.

Most of this book is about how individuals can become more aware of their own less-than-optimal state and change themselves by changing how they respond to stimuli in their lives, including their jobs. Individuals may also change their jobs or their professions. However, no individual change is likely to lead to improvements in the working environment at even one firm, let alone the profession as a whole. Such broader change would have to begin with collective awareness.

It also would require a consensus that change is needed and possible. That in turn would require a willingness to consider the possibility that our ideas about what we are doing and how we are doing it may be incorrect.

Take the common practice (in my experience) of working all night to complete some urgent task or to get through a huge quantity of work. In the short term this leads to a deterioration in the quality of one's work, and in the long term it has significant adverse health effects. Why do we accept this as a rational way to proceed? There seems to be a collective belief that the requirements of the body can be overridden by sheer willpower, and without consequences, or at least without short-term consequences. But even if it is acceptable to subordinate the health of the individual to the profit of the firm, does it make sense to allow, and even encourage, a way of working that results in a lower-quality work product while destroying the well-being of individuals who make up the firm?

The larger belief involved is the old mind–body split: that the mind is separate from—indeed largely independent of—the body, and that the mind is the lawyer's tool, to be used to work and to subdue the needs of the body until the work is done. There is also a strong component of what Alexander called "end-gaining," that is, focusing on the goal so much that one fails to consider whether one has chosen the right means of working toward it. A more modern label for it would be short-term thinking: giving priority to the immediate goal of getting the work done, without considering the longer-term consequences and viability of doing it in a way that ignores one's bodily needs.

The Alexander Technique asks us to stop: to pause long enough before reacting to consider whether in our headlong rush to do something, we are actually doing what we want to do, in the way that is best and most efficient to do it. This is antithetical to the approach to work cultivated in big law firms, where saying yes to every request for help, and responding instantly to every communication, are expected.

Very few of my lawyer students can use the Alexander skill of inhibition in their early lessons. I will discuss with a student, and she will accept, the premise that when I ask her to do something (e.g., to go from sitting to standing), she should not immediately do it, but rather take time to consider whether and how to respond. I then ask her to stand up, and before I have finished the phrase, she is on her feet. It's funny, but also poignant: the embodiment of years of immediate compliance with every demand. With a little practice, my students learn to pause before reacting in lessons. Carrying this new habit over into the outside world is harder though, since everyone else is caught up in the frenzy.

The Alexander Technique also asks us to consider that our habitual way of doing things may seem right, not because it is right, but simply because it is habitual. And it asks us to try consciously choosing a different way, as an experiment, and to be open to learning from the experience.

My students frequently react with surprise when I help them do a simple movement or task with less muscle tension than they habitually apply, and exclaim at how "easy" it seemed. The sensation of a certain amount of work in their muscles tells them how hard they are working, and hence—in their interpretation—how hard the task is. When they accomplish the same task with less perceived effort, it seems that suddenly the task has become easier. To most people, making the tasks of daily life easier seems like a positive change. But from time to time, the feeling of effortlessness provokes some negative reaction. For example, I remember a time when a student who had let go of a great deal of tension in ten minutes of table work got up, walked around, and told me that feeling that free and relaxed made her feel afraid.

Similarly, it is common, in my observation, for lawyers to believe that working at a high level must feel intense, difficult, stressful and exhausting—and the reverse, that work that feels easy must be either slipshod or not challenging enough for prestige. They associate feeling stressed out and exhausted so closely with doing their best work that they actually cultivate the feeling and cannot tolerate calmness in themselves or in colleagues.

Many years ago, the general counsel of a prominent financial services company remarked to me that the job of a lawyer is to worry on behalf of the client. If "worry" is defined as calmly considering everything that might go wrong, and planning to avoid or deal with it, this seems both true and useful. However, many lawyers I know "worry" in the sense of being perpetually anxious. In some cases, the anxiety is evident on the surface and can be very contagious. In fact, I often had the sense, when working with my more overtly anxious colleagues, that they wanted me to display the same anxiety as they did: if I appeared calm, they seemed to think that I was not as serious about the task at hand as they were and to try to provoke me into exhibiting more anxiety. One of my partners once actually remarked to me that he thought a colleague did not deserve to be made partner because he looked so relaxed that he couldn't possibly be serious or hardworking enough.

In other cases, a lawyer's underlying anxiety is expressed as arrogance or aggression. This can be used as a tool when dealing with adversaries, but is just as often directed at colleagues and subordinates. The partner who is always criticizing his peers behind their backs seeks in this way to reassure himself that he is more competent or more diligent than they are. The senior associate who screams at a junior associate for not spotting a typographical error in a document is herself fearful of similar criticism from the partner who supervises them both. The senior lawyer who promises a client to do a project in an unreasonably short period of time, then loses his temper when the colleague who must actually take on the project says she is too busy to comply, is afraid of losing the client to another firm.

But I believe our best thinking—our best work—does not happen when we are anxious. This truth is easier to perceive from the outside. Just as a group of drunken people do not perceive their own conduct in the same way as a sober observer, a group of colleagues who are all frantic and stressed may not perceive how this state of being adversely affects their performance and that of their subordinates.

Fear is not the most effective way of motivating people to perform their best. No one who is hired as a lawyer at a major law firm arrives with a bad work ethic; you cannot acquire the necessary credentials if you are unwilling to do what is necessary to do an outstanding job. In fact, most lawyers I know have an innate desire to excel; being subjected to other people's anxiety and temper tantrums tends to discourage them rather than the opposite. And yet anyone who has worked at a big law firm knows as well as I do that a substantial minority of lawyers inflict their anxiety and bad tempers on everyone around them, and they are unlikely to hear any criticism on this score unless they have some other perceived deficiencies, such as an inability to get and retain clients.

Learning the Alexander Technique has enabled me to deal better with angry, aggressive, and anxious people. It helps me identify my own automatic responses—holding my breath, tensing my neck and shoulders, tightening my jaw—and undo them. It helps me avoid amplifying the other person's negative emotions by mirroring them myself. Sometimes this can defuse the tension in the room and have a positive effect on everyone. But whether it succeeds or not, it feels like a heavy burden on me, requiring a great deal of energy on my part, like fending off an attack.

I used to think, naively, that these problems would all be solved if only everyone took Alexander Technique lessons. Interaction with my fellow teachers and our professional organizations taught me that even experienced Alexander teachers are still human, still have their anxieties, tempers, and internecine feuds and jealousies. However, I still believe that the tools the technique teaches have the potential to improve our individual and collective lives if we have the presence of mind to use them.

So I challenge you, the next time you feel "stressed out" and think you haven't a moment to spare, to take a moment anyway, and stop, be still and silent while becoming fully aware of your entire being (physical, mental, emotional); let your breath out and allow it to come back in; and then consider not just what to do, but how to best do it. And the next time you find yourself part of a team, a meeting, or an organization that seems driven more by anxiety and a mania for speed than by thought, see if you can speak up for a pause, a moment of calm, followed by some rational reflection on the best means to accomplish the group's tasks or goals. If you can do these things, you will be practicing the Alexander Technique.

APPENDIX 1

Alexander Technique Skills and Basic Concepts

Alexander Technique Skills

Awareness: Noticing and describing my habitual movement patterns and the new experiences I have in my lessons and in between lessons. For example, is my neck tightening when I get up from my chair, when I work at my computer, or when I exercise?

Inhibition: Pausing before reacting to a stimulus, whether it comes from outside me or within me. For example, when my cell phone rings, I can pause for a moment before I pick it up to answer. In this pause, I may become aware of what my muscles "want" to do to answer the phone in my habitual way. It also gives me time to give myself a little direction (see below).

Direction: Thinking to myself:

> I allow my neck to be free;
> So that my head can release forward and up (away from the top of my spine);
> So that my torso can lengthen and widen;
> So that my knees can release forward and away from my torso;
> So that my heels can release back and down;
> So that my neck can be free. . . . etc.

Direction is not checking to see if these things are happening, or moving body parts to "make" them change. It's just a light, wishful thought that I renew frequently.

Nondoing: Inhibition is literally "nondoing"—pausing before responding to a stimulus, long enough to consider whether and how to react. Directing is also not doing something, at least not in the way most of us experience "doing." No deliberate muscle action is involved. I may notice my muscles responding to my thoughts, but my primary attention is given to sending the thought, not to trying to do or feel something.

Alexander Technique Basic Concepts

Mind–Body Unity: The mind, brain, and body are not separate. Through the nervous system, which links the brain to the rest of the body, they influence one another constantly. Our thoughts and emotions profoundly affect our bodies, and vice versa.

Good Use of the Self: This is Alexander's term for what we are working toward: fluid, efficient, and alert functioning of body and mind. We talk about the "self" because we are concerned with the whole person, recognizing that body and mind are not separate. We talk about how we "use" ourselves to indicate that we can make conscious choices about how to do our daily activities, so that the cumulative effects of unconscious habits don't cause us pain and dysfunction.

Primary Control: If the head, neck, and back are contracted together, movement is restricted; if the neck is free and the head poised easily, movement becomes more fluid and requires less effort. Thus, the relationship among the head, neck, and back is the key to good coordination and efficient functioning.

Habit and Debauched Kinaesthesia: The force of habit is extremely strong and cannot necessarily be overcome by sheer willpower. When we are used to moving, sitting, and standing in a particular habitual way, it feels wrong to move, sit, and stand differently. The feeling sense may not provide us accurate information about what we are doing. Alexander called this phenomenon "debauched kinaesthesia," or "unreliable sensory appreciation."

Means-Whereby vs. End-Gaining: If we keep concentrating on a goal, we may fail to give attention to how we can best attain the goal. Alexander called excessive focus on the goal as "end-gaining." Students of the Alexander Technique practice letting go of this attitude and replacing it with an attention to the means they use to attain their goal—the "means-whereby" in Alexander's terminology. We practice this using very simple goals: for example, getting in and out of a chair while giving attention to not tightening the neck.

Don't Take a Deep Breath: Efficient, easy breathing begins with breathing out. An in-breath will follow automatically; there is no need to "take a breath."

APPENDIX 2

Teacher Training Standards and How to Find a Teacher

F.M. Alexander trained a number of teachers in his work during the latter part of his life, in London, and they in turn trained others, who trained others, and so on. Some members of the first generation of teachers trained by Alexander himself founded the Society of Teachers of the Alexander Technique (STAT) in London. STAT has established standards for training and certifying Alexander Technique teachers. The standards of STAT and its affiliates around the world, including the American Society for the Alexander Technique (AmSAT), call for training courses based on 1,600 hours of instruction, generally over a 3-year period. My own training took place at the American Center for the Alexander Technique (ACAT) in New York, whose teacher training program (the oldest in the United States) meets the AmSAT requirements.

There are skilled teachers of the technique who have not been certified in accordance with the standards of STAT and AmSAT. However, for those who are seeking a teacher in the United States without the benefit of a personal referral, I recommend seeking out an AmSAT-certified teacher.

AmSAT's website includes a listing of teachers that is searchable by geographic area, as well as general information about the Alexander Technique: http://www.amsatonline.org

ACAT's website includes a listing of teachers in the New York metropolitan area, divided geographically, including by specific neighborhoods in Manhattan: http://www.acatnyc.org/main/

Index

7912 NW 137th Ave
Morriston, FL.
32668